THINK ABOUT IT!

PROJECTS AND PUZZLES
FOR ALL THE FAMILY

Written by Ian Howarth

Julian Messner
Parsippany, New Jersey

Illustrated by
Robert Farnworth, Mick Gillah, Chris Lyons, Steve Noon, Tony Smith, Paul Thorley and Lynne Willey,
and at Specs Art: Shantal Freeman, Gillian Hunt, Roger Jones, Don Simpson, Gerald Witcomb.

Picture credits
AOL   Andromeda Oxford Ltd.
SPL   Science Photo Library
6tl AOL; **6cl** AOL; **6-7** Gamma Press/Frank Spooner Pictures; **8tr** Newbury Weekly News; **8-9** Images Colour
Library; **11tr** AOL x3; **12** Bill Redic Photography; **15** Clive Brunskill/Allsport; **16-17** Pictor International; **18**
James King-Holmes/ SPL; **24cr** Nicola Sutton/Life File; **24-5** Steve Etherington/ Empics; **25cr** AOL; **29** AOL; **30tr**
Mary Evans Picture Library; **30bl** National Medical Slide Bank; **30br** Alex Bartel/SPL; **41** Argos; **42** AOL x3.
The publishers would also like to thank Dr. John Raven for permission to use the two matrices that appear on
page 23.

Planned and produced by
Andromeda Oxford Limited
11-15 The Vineyard
Abingdon
Oxon
OX14 3PX
England

Copyright © Andromeda Oxford Limited 1996

Published in 1997 in the United States by

Julian Messner
A Division of Simon & Schuster
299 Jefferson Road
Parsippany, New Jersey 07054-0480

Library of Congress Cataloging-in-Publication Data
Howarth, Ian.
Think about it!: activities to show you how people think/by Ian Howarth.
p.   cm. --(Amazing brain series)
Summary: Explains the underlying scientific principles behind the way humans think and solve problems,
through a series of self-tests and puzzles.
1. Thought and thinking--Juvenile literature. 2. Thought and thinking--Testing--Juvenile literature. 3. Human information
processing--Juvenile literature. [1. Thought and thinking. 2. Memory. 3. Brain.] I. Title. II. Series: Howarth, Ian
1928- . Amazing Brain
BF441.G73   1996   96-6976
153.4'2--dc20   CIP
                                                     AC

ISBN 0-382-39603-0 (LSB) 1 2 3 4 5 6 7 8 9 10
ISBN 0-382-39604-9 (pbk) 1 2 3 4 5 6 7 8 9 10

PRINTED IN BELGIUM BY

INTERNATIONAL BOOK PRODUCTION

Contents

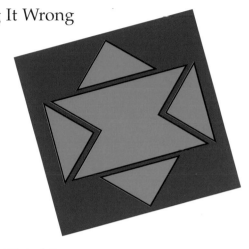

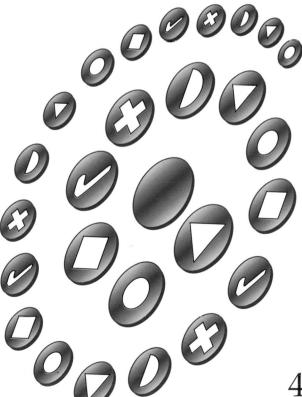

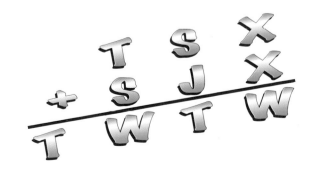

What Is Thinking?

Imagining, planning, calculating, understanding others, solving problems, checking if you are right—all these things are thinking.

THERE ARE MANY DIFFERENT KINDS OF THINKING. We may think alone or with other people, either in cooperation or in competition. We may calculate with numbers, reason with words, or imagine things as a mental picture. Quick thinking, which often includes reacting quickly, is another thinking skill. Memory is important too, because without it we can only think about the things in front of us. When cooperating, it is important to understand the other person's thinking so that we can learn from them or teach them. All these types of thinking are used in complex activities such as the mountain rescue operation shown here. And they are also required for the Brain Games below and on the following pages. When we are in competition with someone, it is important to try and anticipate what the opponent is thinking, in order to avoid any traps they might set.

Brain Games

REMEMBER THE ROUTE

Look at this collection of objects (left) for ten seconds and memorize the position of each one. Close your eyes and ask a friend to name any two objects on the edge of the picture. Can you name all the objects on the shortest route between the two? You can also use your own objects, moving them between each turn.

WHICH SWITCH?

There are three switches outside a closed door (above) and three light bulbs inside the room. How could you work out which switch operates each light bulb, if you are only allowed to switch on and switch off two of the switches before going into the room? (Turn to the Answers pages to find out.)

FILLING KNOWLEDGE GAPS

Each shape (right) stands for a number. These add up to give the numbers down the side and along the bottom. What number does each shape stand for and what is the missing number? Could you find it without cracking the code? (Find out on the Answers pages.)

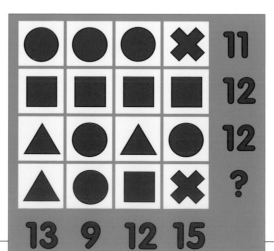

WORKING AS A TEAM ▼

The team leader (in red) is anticipating what the victim has done. He has advised the assistant (in green) what instructions to give the volunteers, taking into account their different abilities. The navigator (in blue) is calculating distances and times on the map.

Speeds

	flat ground	3 mph
>	up slight hill	2 mph
>>	up steep hill	1 mph
<	down slight hill	4 mph
<<	down steep hill	5 mph

15 m
8 m
12 m
5 m
g
5 m
j
f
x
8 m
5 m
6 m
Home

RAT IN A TRAP

This game for two people tests how quick your reactions are. Fill an old sock with sand and tie a knot in the tail to make a "rat." One player drops the rat down a cardboard tube and the other has to hit it hard as it comes out (left). The "dropper" can try to make it easy or difficult for the hitter.

FIND THE QUICKEST ROUTE

A rescue team thinks the injured party is at either the red or the blue flag on the map above. Which route should they take in order to reach both sites in the shortest time? The distances are marked on the map and the speeds up- and downhill are shown in the table and marked as arrows on the map. What advantage would there be in sending out two teams? (See Answers pages.)

Getting It Right and Getting It Wrong

It isn't always possible to look up the answer to a problem. Often trial and error is the only way to test if an idea will work.

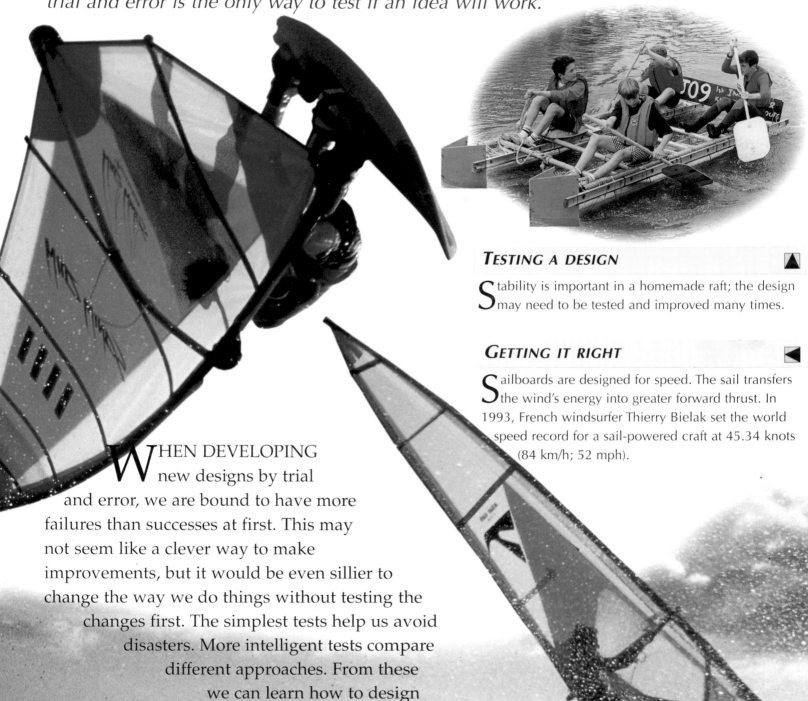

TESTING A DESIGN ▲

Stability is important in a homemade raft; the design may need to be tested and improved many times.

GETTING IT RIGHT ◄

Sailboards are designed for speed. The sail transfers the wind's energy into greater forward thrust. In 1993, French windsurfer Thierry Bielak set the world speed record for a sail-powered craft at 45.34 knots (84 km/h; 52 mph).

WHEN DEVELOPING new designs by trial and error, we are bound to have more failures than successes at first. This may not seem like a clever way to make improvements, but it would be even sillier to change the way we do things without testing the changes first. The simplest tests help us avoid disasters. More intelligent tests compare different approaches. From these we can learn how to design even better ways of doing things.

Brain Games

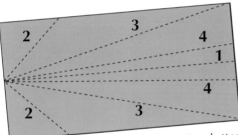

WHAT IS THE LONGEST SPAN?

You can make surprisingly wide bridges from playing cards. In this simple one (right), there is just less than a card's length between each support. Can you design one that spans a much greater gap without using glue or tape? (See Answers pages.)

DESIGNING PAPER PLANES

Below are the designs for the fighter (swept-back wings) and the glider (long, thin wings) shown above. Try them out, then design your own planes.

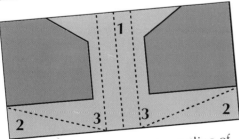

Fighter: Fold the paper along the dotted lines. Fold 1, 2, and 3 inward and fold 4 outward. Swept-back wings are fast and easier to control than thin wings.

Glider. Step one: Draw the outline of the glider (above) on a piece of paper. Turn the paper over and fold 1 and 2 inward along the dotted lines.

Step two: Cut out the shaded area and fold 3 outward. Thin-winged planes stay up longer but are hard to control. Attaching paper clips to the nose will help.

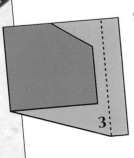

DESIGN A SPINNER

The design of a paper helicopter is not as obvious to many people as a paper glider. But "spinners" can stay up just as long as paper planes. All you need is a sheet of paper, a pencil, some scissors and a paper clip to use as a weight (below and right). Hint: think of a helicopter often seen in nature! See if you can design your own before turning to the Answers pages for one design.

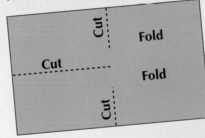

A CODING DEVICE

The disk on the right can be used for both coding and decoding messages. Write a message in code by finding each letter on the outer ring and replacing it with the corresponding letter on the inner ring. To decode, reverse the process. Anyone with the same disk can decode your messages. Or you can design your own disk. How could you make it more difficult for someone without the disk to decode the message but still easy for someone with the disk? (See the Answers pages.)

What Are Brains For?

Some parts of our brains take in information, and other parts process the information received.

PROBABLY THE FIVE MOST IMPORTANT functions of the brain are: sensing the environment, communication, recognition, instructing the body to move, and thinking or reasoning. (Each Brain Game on the next page falls into one of these categories.) We know from recordings made of activity in the brain that the five senses—vision, hearing, smell, taste, and touch—all send messages to different parts of the brain. Other parts are involved in coordinating movement. And still other parts are more specialized, such as the area necessary for understanding speech and the area used in producing speech. Large parts of the brain have no distinct function but may be involved in many different kinds of thinking, causing bursts of electrical energy to surge through the brain. Scientists have also learned a lot about how the brain works by studying the loss of brain function after accidents or strokes.

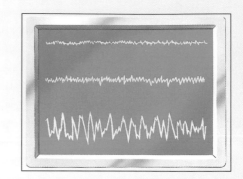

BRAIN WAVES ▲

The amount of electrical activity in your brain—recorded as "brain waves"—gives a rough indication of the speed of your thinking. When you think hard, they are fast and irregular (top row). They slow down as you get drowsy (middle row), and are long and slow when you are asleep (bottom row).

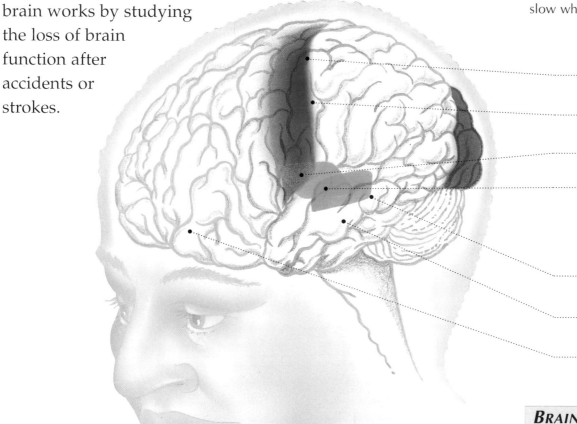

Movement of legs

Movement of trunk

Movement of head

Speech overlaps the movement and hearing areas, usually in the left half of the brain in right-handed people.

Hearing

Memory (inside)

Thinking and personality

BRAIN POWER ◄

This picture shows the location of areas of the brain responsible for various functions.

Brain Games

TWO THINGS AT ONCE

Because of the way the brain is organized, some movements are easy to do by themselves but very difficult to do in combination with other movements. Can you pat your head and rub your stomach (left) at the same time? Now try locking your fingers together and rotating your thumbs in opposite directions!

SALTY, SWEET, SOUR, OR BITTER?

You can map these four main taste sensations on your tongue (right). Place a tiny bit of salt on the tip of your tongue. If you recognize a salty taste, mark SA (for SAlty) on a drawing of your tongue at the tip. Now put some in the middle, then on the back and sides of your tongue, and note the result. Rinse your mouth and repeat with sugar (SWeet), lemon juice (SOur), and dried coffee (BItter). Compare your map with the one on the Answers pages.

WHAT IS THE MISSING CARD?

Take a pack of cards, fan them out facedown, and ask a friend to pull out a card without saying what it is. How many times do you need to look through the face-up pack to find out which card is missing? Hint: there are only two colors and four suits in a pack, with 13 cards in each suit. Remember that **every** card has, or can be given, a numerical value. (See the Answers pages for one solution.)

RECOGNITION

Can you identify the three objects (below), photographed either close up or from an unusual angle? See the Answers pages.

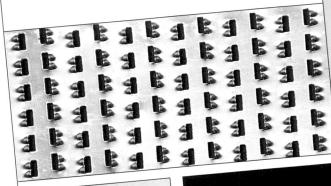

COMMUNICATION

When you draw a picture, the visual brain communicates with the part of the brain that controls movement. But can your visual brain direct a friend's movements? Sit back-to-back with a friend and describe an object to him/her without saying what it is (below). Your friend should try and draw the object. Take turns and see who is better. It's hard because the part of the brain that controls speech is not very good at dealing with visual space.

Is the Brain a Computer?

Computers do many things better than we can, and they are improving at others; but our brains still do some things better than computers.

SIMPLE COMPUTERS DO ONLY what we instruct them to, in "programmed" languages that work a little like our own. They can't recognize faces or read messy handwriting, but they calculate much better than we can. More advanced types are being designed to be more like the human brain; they can recognize some faces and understand simple instructions given in our language. They can also learn from experience. A computer would find the two calculating Brain Games on the next page easier than you will, but you will be better at the other three! Try them and see.

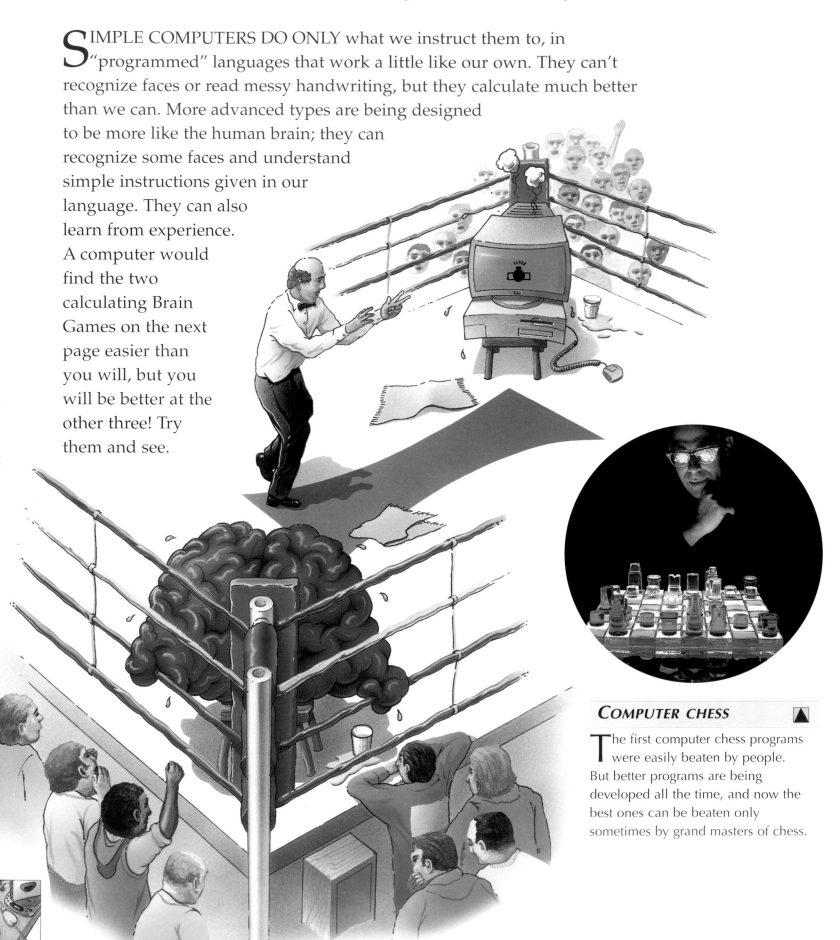

COMPUTER CHESS ▲

The first computer chess programs were easily beaten by people. But better programs are being developed all the time, and now the best ones can be beaten only sometimes by grand masters of chess.

Brain Games

$$\begin{array}{r} T \\ + \ T \\ \hline T \end{array} \quad \begin{array}{r} S \\ S \\ \hline W \end{array} \quad \begin{array}{r} S \\ J \\ \hline T \end{array} \quad \begin{array}{r} X \\ X \\ \hline W \end{array}$$

$Fe_4[Fe(CN)_6]_3$
$Na_2SiO_4 \cdot xH_2O$
$CaSO_4 \cdot \frac{1}{2}H_2O$

CRYPTARITHMETIC

Cryptarithmetic is arithmetic in code. What numbers do the letters above stand for, given that X = 5 ? Some clever tricks can be used to solve this kind of problem, but people generally fall back on trial and error, which computers do much faster than people. (Check your answer on the Answers pages.)

READING BAD HANDWRITING

Can you read these chemical formulas (above), despite the bad handwriting? A computer can display bad handwriting on its screen but it can't interpret the information like we can. (See Answers pages.)

CRACK THE PRICE CODE

Some storekeepers put coded prices on their goods (right and below). Can you crack the code and work out the price of each of the six items? A computer could do this very quickly. (See Answers pages.)

M.NL

K.RQ

$4.96

K.RQ

$3.76

N.KK

L.ST

$3.22

L.PN

N.PL

$2.82

1 **2** **3**

4 **5** **6**

MATCHING FACES

Look at the faces above. They belong to three boys (there are two pictures of each boy). Can you identify which pictures are the same boy? Match the numbers and check your answers on the Answers pages. This kind of test is very difficult for computers.

HOW GOOD IS YOUR MEMORY?

This game is the most fun when played competitively. Study the objects on the tray (right) for 30 seconds and try to memorize them. Now turn away and write down as many as you can. Is your memory better than your friend's memory? A computer could store the list of objects in its memory until you removed it. But it could not put names to each object without help.

What Will They Do Next?

Whether competing against someone or cooperating with them, we need to know what the other person is going to do next.

IN ALL KINDS OF SITUATIONS, it is very important to know what the other person is thinking so that we can predict their next move. But it isn't always easy. If someone always thinks or does the same thing, you can predict that they will do it again. But if they vary their actions, you need to look for some pattern in their behavior or a motive behind it. In cooperative activities, such as ballet or paired figure skating, it is essential for both people to share precise information about every move they make. But in competitive games such as football or card games, one player may deliberately try to mislead the opponents. Team members may also send coded signals to each other, which the opposition will try and interpret so that the next move does not catch them off guard.

Brain Games

CHEAT!

Deal out all the cards to three or more players (below). Player One puts one to four cards of the same kind face down and says what cards he/she is playing e.g. one to four Queens, but they **can** cheat! Player Two either puts down one to four cards immediately above or below Queens (or can also state he/she is putting down one to four Queens), or accuses Player One of cheating. The accused player must turn over his/her cards. If he/she cheated, the player picks up all the cards on the table. If he/she did not, the accuser picks them up. The game goes on until one player has no cards left.

WHICH BARBER?

John is on vacation in a small town miles from anywhere. There are only two barbers in town (above). The first is messy and he has a terrible haircut. The second is tidy and he has a neat haircut. Which barber should John go to and why? (Look up the answer on the Answers pages at the back of the book.)

ANTICIPATING THE PLAY ▶

In a soccer match, an attacking player often tries to bluff the goalkeeper into defending a particular side of the net, while he/she kicks the ball into the other side. The goalkeeper must try and predict the attacker's next move: will he/she bluff or double bluff?

PICK-UP-STICKS

Take a handful of toothpicks or straws and let them fall in a pile on the table (below). With a friend, take turns removing one straw at a time from the pile. If you move any of the other straws, you miss a turn. The winner is the person who picks up the most straws.

RED AND BLUE STICKERS

Show two friends that you have one red sticker and two blue ones. Ask them to shut their eyes, then stick a blue sticker on each friend's forehead. Tell them to open their eyes (right). They should be able to work out the color of their own sticker without taking it off, asking any questions or looking in a mirror. How? (See Answers pages.)

GUESS THE RULE

The dealer invents a rule that the other players must work out through trial and error (for example, any red card must be followed by a black card, or the next card played must be two higher than the last card played). The dealer writes down the rule and keeps it hidden. All the cards are dealt, and the players take turns to play a card face up (above). If their card follows the secret rule, the dealer lets it lie. If it does not, it is returned to the player, who puts it in a separate pile and cannot play it again. The winner is the player with least cards returned.

Are You Right For the Job?

*Different jobs suit different kinds of people. Simple tests can show what your abilities are and what sorts of jobs might suit **you**!*

SOME PEOPLE KNOW EXACTLY WHAT THEY WANT to do when they grow up. Their vocation might be to work with animals, people, machines, or computers. Others find it very hard to know, partly because they have not had a chance to find out what they are really good at. To help them, all kinds of tests have been developed in the form of games, questions, and puzzles. These test a person's ability in a wide range of skills important to different jobs, such as mathematical ability, concentration, and attention to detail. Some people find details fascinating, but others are bored by them, responding better to the broad outlines of a task. How do you respond? Do you persevere until you have understood all the small details of a problem, or do you give up in despair? The Brain Games on these pages are examples of tests used to assess your abilities in different areas.

Brain Games

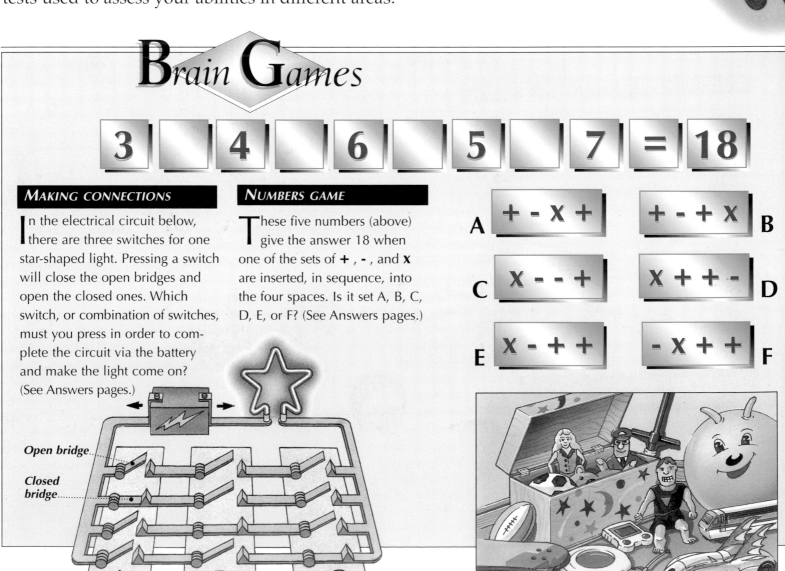

MAKING CONNECTIONS

In the electrical circuit below, there are three switches for one star-shaped light. Pressing a switch will close the open bridges and open the closed ones. Which switch, or combination of switches, must you press in order to complete the circuit via the battery and make the light come on? (See Answers pages.)

NUMBERS GAME

These five numbers (above) give the answer 18 when one of the sets of **+** , **-** , and **x** are inserted, in sequence, into the four spaces. Is it set A, B, C, D, E, or F? (See Answers pages.)

3   4   6   5   7 = 18

A + - x +   + - + x B

C x - - +   x + + - D

E x - + +   - x + + F

Open bridge
Closed bridge

A   B   C

Abilities	Poor	Excellent
• language		
• math		
• spatial ability		
• manual skills		
• social skills		

ABILITY PROFILE ▲

How you respond to tests like the Brain Games below depends on your abilities in five main areas (above). Such a profile can help suggest a suitable career. This one suggests someone who might be good at computer programming.

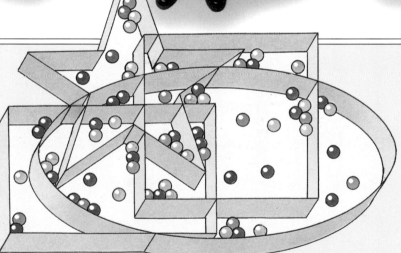

ATTENTION TO DETAIL

Many jobs require a good eye for detail. How detail conscious are you? Write down how many little balls there are in the star, the square, the oval, and the rectangle (above). How many balls are there altogether? (See Answers pages.)

SPOT THE DIFFERENCE

Can you spot the 12 things that are different in these two pictures (left and far left)? What are they? (Turn to the Answers pages to find out.)

WHAT COMES NEXT?

Which of the shapes labeled 1 to 5 comes next in the sequence (top)? And which of the shapes labeled A to E completes the box (above)? (See Answers pages.)

Could You Be a Pilot?

Pilots must pass many tests during training. Some of these tests are like the Brain Games on the opposite page.

TRAINING A PILOT IS VERY EXPENSIVE, so air forces and commercial airlines only train the most able people. To find out who is most able, they ask the candidates to take aptitude tests—similar to these Brain Games— which are designed to help select the people with the right skills for being a pilot. The tests show how good each candidate is at the sorts of skills needed for flying an aircraft. These include following complex instructions, ignoring distractions, being able to keep calm in emergencies, and handling the controls accurately.

At the beginning of training, mistakes can be made by even the best trainees. So to avoid accidents, much of the early training takes place in computer-operated flight simulators that are just like the real thing, except that they never leave the ground.

COMPUTERIZED FLIGHT ◄

Flight simulators are like very big and very expensive computer games. You may possibly have tried a small flight simulator on a home computer, but the professional flight simulators used in training pilots give almost all-around vision, and the cockpit can move up and down and roll around to re-create the sensation of flying a real plane. Strapped into their seats, the trainee pilots learn to move the controls accurately and make quick decisions in safety; and if there is a crash in the simulator, at least no one gets hurt.

Brain Games

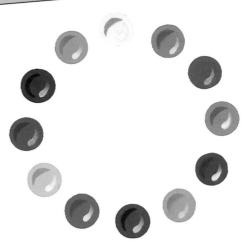

AGILE EYES

Trace this ring of circles (right). Move a pen from the top circle to the circle one place to the right. Then move two places right, bypassing one circle, then three places right, bypassing two circles, and so on, bypassing one more circle each move. Compete with a friend to see who can make the most moves in ten seconds.

HIDDEN TRIANGLES

Pilots sometimes have to spot objects on the ground that are not easy to see at first. How many triangles can you see in this picture (left)? There are probably more than you think! (See Answers pages.)

SIDEWAYS GLANCE

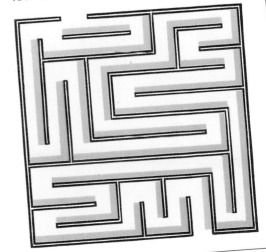

A pilot must be able to recognize landmarks from unusual angles. To an untrained eye, this can be hard. What does the shape above look like? Check by rotating the book 90 degrees clockwise.

EYE-MAZING

Trace this maze (below) onto paper. Use a pencil to follow a path through the maze without touching the sides. Time yourself and count how many times your pencil touches the sides of the maze. It should take about 10 seconds. Touching the sides less than four times shows good coordination.

LEFT, RIGHT, LEFT?

Each of these men (above) is holding a baton in one hand. You must decide whether the baton is in the left or the right hand. Write the numbers 1 to 18 on a sheet of paper. Against the number representing each figure, put a letter "L" for those holding the baton in the left hand, and a letter "R" for those holding it in the right hand. Time yourself to see how long it takes. Look at the Answers pages to see if you made any mistakes. Finishing the task in 20 seconds with less than three mistakes is good.

How Quickly Can You Think?

Quick thinking and fast reactions are important in many sports and in some jobs, such as flying jet airplanes.

ARE YOU A FAST OR SLOW THINKER? It depends on what kind of person you are, on how much practice you have had, and on whether you can find clever ways to simplify your thinking. It also depends on the difficulty of the task you are performing (although this affects everyone almost equally), the time of day, your mood, how hungry you are, and how short of sleep you are. The Brain Games opposite test not only your ability to think quickly, but also your power of concentration and the speed of your hand-to-eye coordination. Compare your speeds with those of your friends, or try to get faster with practice and by using clever thinking tricks.

Brain Games

QUICK SORTING

The more types of a thing you have to think about, the slower your reactions become. Count the number of objects on the left. How long does it take? Now count how many red and how may green shapes there are (i.e. 2 different types of an object). This takes longer. Now count how many red triangles, green triangles, red circles, and green circles there are (4 different types). This takes longer still. Count how many of each of the four types have dots (8 different types), then find out how many of these have shadows (16 different types). The more types of a thing you have to count, the longer it takes, although each time you only consider 30 objects altogether. (Correct counts are given on the Answers pages, and a suggestion to make counting easier.)

A COUNTING-BACKWARD RACE

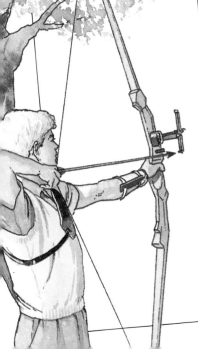

Distractions slow your thinking. Practice makes it faster. Count backward in threes from 100 (97, 94, 91. . .) down to 10. It will take about a minute (left). But with practice you can do it in less than 30 seconds. Challenge a friend to a race. Because you have practiced you will probably win easily, even if your friend tries to distract you!

STOP THE RULER!

Measure your fastest reactions. Ask a friend to press a ruler vertically against a wall. Hold your hand near the bottom of the ruler about half an inch from the wall. When the friend drops the ruler, stop it by pushing it against the wall. The faster you react, the smaller the distance it will fall. To measure your speed, trace the scale on page 43 and stick it to the ruler, then line up the zero with a mark on the wall.

HIT THE TARGETS AS FAST AS YOU CAN!

The more accurate your hand-to-eye coordination has to be, the slower you become. Trace the four bull's-eyes (below) onto paper, keeping the same distances between them. Move a pencil as fast as possible back and forth between the two larger ones. Time yourself making fifty moves. Repeat the exercise with the two smaller bull's-eyes. How much longer does it take?

Boys and Girls

Do you think boys and girls are naturally good at doing different things? Or do you think it is just a matter of practice?

BOYS AND GIRLS SOMETIMES HAVE different interests, abilities, and ambitions. Girls often seem to be a little better with words and with people, boys with numbers, objects, and spatial relationships. But tests show that any differences in ability between boys and girls are in fact very small, and what differences there are may be entirely due to different interests and experiences. The difference in ability between boys and girls is much less than the range of ability within each sex.

You can also find out things about your personality by examining your immediate reaction to these games. Strong-willed or stubborn people—both girls and boys—tend to practice the things they find difficult until they become good at them. But most of us spend more time doing things we are already good at.

Brain Games

TURNING THE COGS

Here are three sets of cog wheels (below). If you turn the first cogs in the direction of the arrows, will the two buckets on A go up or down, and will the last cogs of B and C turn clockwise or counterclockwise? Write down your answers and check them on the Answers pages.

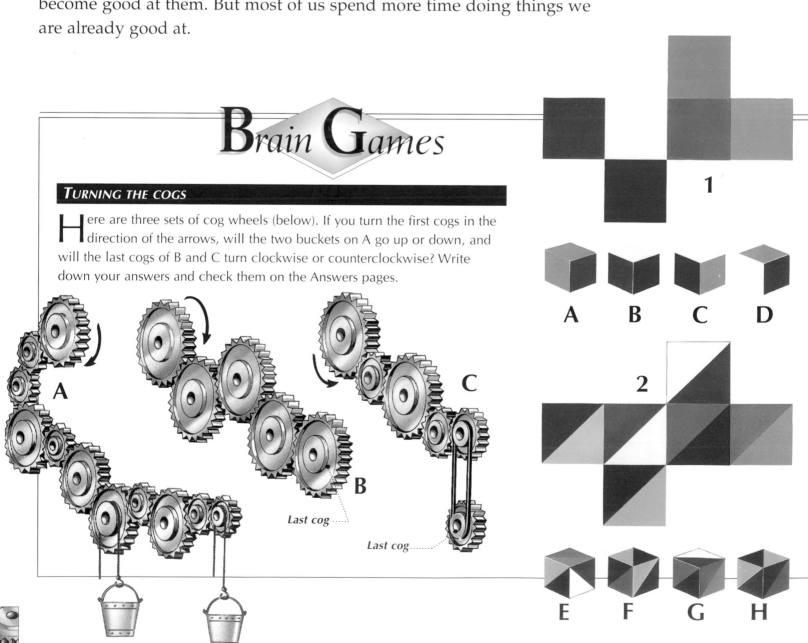

A   B   C   D

Last cog

Last cog

1

2

E   F   G   H

SPELLING TEST

What is the eleven-letter word that all college graduates spell incorrectly? Try this one on your friends before turning to the Answers pages!

MAKING BOXES

Which box—A, B, C, or D (top left)—can you make from cardboard cutout number 1, and which box—E, F, G, or H (left)—from cardboard cutout number 2? (Answers on the Answers pages.)

NEXT IN THE SEQUENCE

Look at the two sets of eight shapes above. In each set, the pattern of shapes changes in such a way that you should be able to work out the missing ninth shape. For each set, is it box A, B, C, D, E, F, G, or H? (See Answers pages.)

Does Practice Make Perfect?

It usually does, but it has to be the right kind of practice.

NO MATTER HOW smart you are, you can't become an expert at something like chess or playing a musical instrument without lots of practice. It takes years of practice to become world-class, and the brain needs practice as well as the body. It is usually impossible to practice all of a complicated skill when you start, so you must practice parts of it separately, progressing to the complete task as you improve. But what sort of practice should you do? Imagining doing the task without actually doing it is a surprisingly good form of practice; it helps you avoid mistakes when you do perform the task. Try the Brain Games here and see what kinds of practice help you get better.

HIGH-SPEED THINKING ▼

Even sport superstars as skillful as Formula One racing drivers need to practice, and special sessions are set up for this before each race. Racing drivers often play sports such as tennis, because being physically fit helps them to improve their skills at racing.

KEEPING IT ALL IN THE AIR

Juggling is a case of practice makes perfect. Here's how to do it.

Step one: Start with one ball. Toss it up in the air from the right hand to the left hand, then pass it quickly back to your right hand. Repeat until you can do both things rapidly.

Step two: Next, start with one ball in each hand and while throwing the one in the right hand over to the left hand, pass the one in the left hand to the right hand and continue.

Step three: Now, start with one ball in the right hand and two in the left. If you throw the one in the right hand high enough, you will be able to move both of those in the left hand into the right hand, one after the other, tossing the first into the air before passing the second across. It usually helps to imagine doing it with the extra ball before trying it for real.

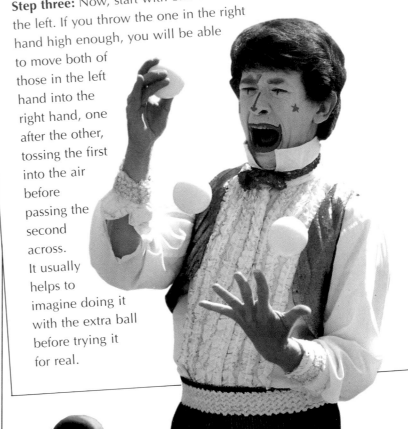

Brain Games

CHINESE WRITING

It takes a lot of practice to learn a new language. Chinese is especially hard because Chinese writing is made up of pictures called characters instead of letters. Each of the characters on the right contains the symbol of either a mountain, a moon, or a heart. Can you pick them all out? (See Answers pages.) Practice copying the characters using a paintbrush and thin black paint. Do you get faster with practice?

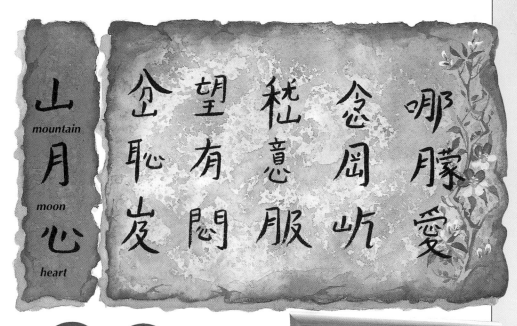

山
mountain

月
moon

心
heart

A

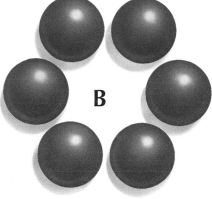

B

MAKE A CIRCLE IN THREE MOVES

Change the shape of A to B (above) by moving only three of the marbles (or you can use coins). The moved marbles must not be picked up, and they must stay close to at least two others after each move. Check your moves on the Answers pages. You may find it difficult even then!

MIRROR MAZE

Draw a maze, like the one above (or copy the one on page 19), and put it behind a screen or book so that you can't see it. Then put a mirror beyond the maze so that you can see its reflection. Follow the path through the maze by looking in the mirror. You will improve rapidly with practice!

Is It Just a Trick?

Sometimes the solution to a puzzle—reached by careful thinking—can look like magic!

THINKING ABOUT WHAT HAPPENS to things when they are turned, bent, or stretched is called topology. It can lead to many surprising effects that look like tricks until you begin to think about shapes more clearly. A pullover sweater has only four holes, no matter how you twist and turn it; a coat has only three holes; and a sock only one. We can do surprising things with our clothes, and with other shapes, when we bend and stretch them. For example, it is possible to take off a vest without taking off your jacket, even though the two garments appear to be linked together when you try.

B*rain* G*ames*

KNIGHT MOVES

Can you make the two red knights and the two yellow knights on this miniature chessboard (below) change places using only "legal" knight moves? The legal moves are shown by the white lines. You must keep to the squares on the chessboard shown here. Only one piece at a time is allowed on any square. You might want to practice with real chess pieces and a real chessboard. (See Answers pages.)

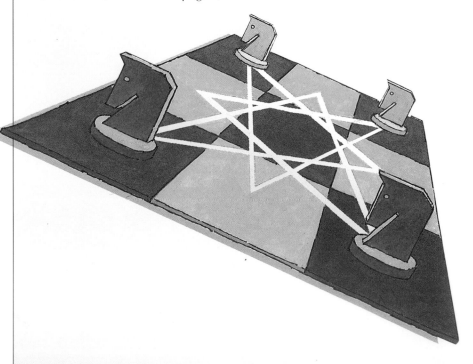

MATCH THE ROTATED SHAPES

Two of the shapes below have been rotated so that you see them from a different angle. Can you match them with the corresponding shapes? Two of the shapes can't be paired up. Which two are they? (Check your answers on the Answers pages.)

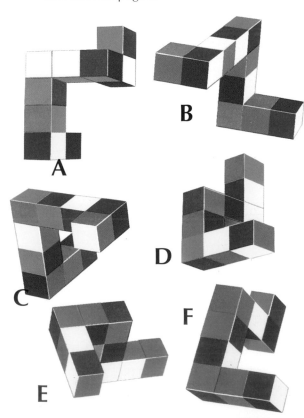

A

B

C

D

E

F

26

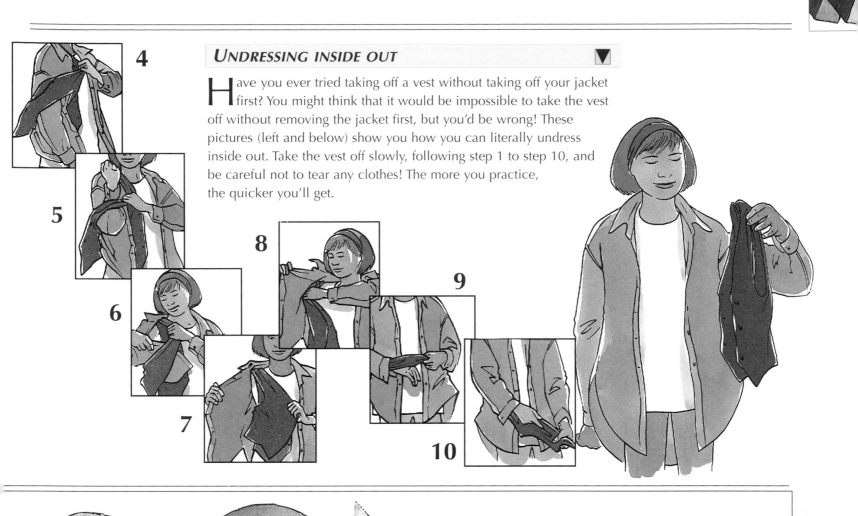

UNDRESSING INSIDE OUT ▼

4

5

6

7

8

9

10

Have you ever tried taking off a vest without taking off your jacket first? You might think that it would be impossible to take the vest off without removing the jacket first, but you'd be wrong! These pictures (left and below) show you how you can literally undress inside out. Take the vest off slowly, following step 1 to step 10, and be careful not to tear any clothes! The more you practice, the quicker you'll get.

ONE-SIDED PAPER

Stick two ends of a piece of paper together with a half twist to make what is known as a Mobius strip (above). What happens if you cut along the middle of the Mobius strip? Two strips of paper make a double Mobius (right). Make one and cut it the same way. What happens? (See Answers pages.)

WHAT KNOT?

The top knot (right) is a reef knot, used to tie sails on a sailboat. The linked loops make it secure. However, by threading one end through the knot, you can unlink the loops so that the knot can be untied by pulling the two ends. This is called a slipknot. Which of the knots on the right (A or B) is a slipknot? (See Answers pages.)

A   **B**

GET UNKNOTTED

Tie yourself to a friend, as shown above. Use long loops, but don't tie them too tightly around your wrists. The two loops seem to be linked, but in fact they are not. How can you separate from each other without untying the knots? (See Answers pages.)

More Tricks

Scientific breakthroughs that challenge conventional ideas are often difficult to accept and can look like tricks.

UNTIL THE 1600's, people thought that different types of objects moved naturally at different speeds. The Italian scientist Galileo Galilei was the first person to suspect that all things move at a constant speed until a force acts upon them. To most people at the time, this was quite unbelievable. Galileo claimed that apart from things like feathers, which are slowed by the resistance of the air, all objects fall at the same rate. He showed he was right by dropping a cannonball and a bullet from the top of the Tower of Pisa at exactly the same moment, and finding that they landed at the same time. Once people realized that force is needed to speed things up or slow them down, they began to understand things like friction and lubrication and could measure the forces exerted by machines. The Brain Games opposite can be solved logically or by trial and error (experiments). Scientists usually make discoveries by a combination of both methods.

GALILEO'S TELESCOPE ▲

In 1609, Galileo looked at the planets through a telescope. He was one of the first people ever to do so. Like the earlier Polish astronomer Nicolaus Copernicus, he concluded that the Earth and the planets move around the Sun. Because this was such a revolutionary idea and against the teachings of the Roman Catholic Church, he was convicted of heresy and was permitted to return to his own house on condition he did not leave it.

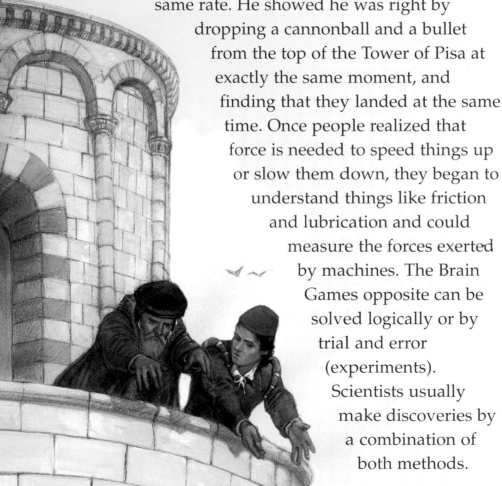

AMAZING DISCOVERIES ◄

Galileo dropped a cannonball and a bullet from the top of the Tower of Pisa at the same moment and both hit the ground together. Later, the English scientist Isaac Newton suggested that the Earth was "pulling" them toward it. At first this was thought nonsensical too!

Brain Games

WHO IS THE TALLEST?

These five boys, numbered one to five (right), are each a different height. Can you work out who the tallest and who the shortest is called if: Peter is taller than Dave, Jack is taller than Alan, Dave is taller than Tom, and Alan is taller than Peter? Write down on a piece of paper the name of Number One and the name of Number Five, then turn to the Answers pages to see if you are right.

1   2   3   4   5

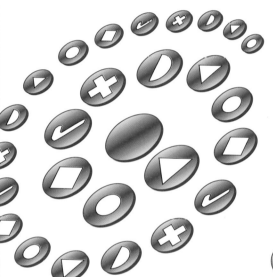

NEXT IN THE SEQUENCE

Which of the six disks labeled A to F below is next in the sequence at the center of the spiral on the left? Think carefully about the pattern of shapes before you decide. (Find out on the Answers pages.)

A   B   C   D   E   F

GUESS-THE-CARD GAME

Look at the 10 cards laid out below. Ignoring the suit, can you work out what the number of the face-down card is? (Check your answer on the Answers pages.)

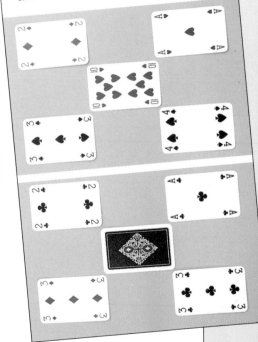

ARE YOUR WIRES CROSSED?

Connect all three utilities—water, electricity, and gas—to each of the three houses (left) without any of the pipes or cables crossing. This one may bend your mind for a long time! (Turn to the Answers pages if desperate.)

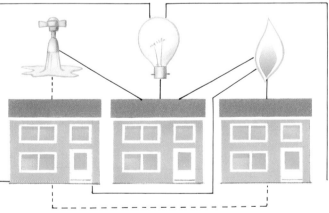

THE SHEEP PEN PUZZLE

The sheep pen on the right is made from 12 hurdles. It is just big enough to hold 6 sheep. If the farmer buys 6 more sheep, how many more hurdles will he need to double the size of the sheep pen? (See Answers pages.)

The Missing Link

One piece of missing information can be all you need to solve a problem, but it isn't always easy to find.

IMPORTANT SCIENTIFIC DISCOVERIES can take scientists many years to make, or they can happen in an instant almost by accident, all because one vital piece of missing information falls into place. And even when an important discovery is made, it can be years before its significance is understood. A Scottish doctor, Alexander Fleming, spent most of his life in a laboratory looking for ways to kill bacteria, the germs that cause many infections and can result in death. One day in 1928, when he was experimenting with a particular bacterium, he noticed that it did not multiply near some mold that was growing on the jelly, or culture, on which he was growing the bacteria. The mold, called *Penicillium*, produced a substance that killed bacteria. About twenty years passed before other scientists extracted antibiotics from mold in order to treat infections.

ANTISEPTIC BREAKTHROUGH ▲

Until the late 1800's, many people died after operations because nobody knew that germs cause disease. The English surgeon Joseph Lister first saw the link. He discovered that after washing his hands in carbolic acid, cuts did not become infected. Lister's antiseptic carbolic spray, used during surgery (above), saved countless lives.

ANTIBIOTICS ◄ ▼

The bluish-gray areas of mold on this loaf of bread are the fungus *Penicillium*, some species of which are used to produce the antibiotic penicillin. On the culture in the petrie dish (left), the areas free of bacteria surround places where an antibiotic has been applied.

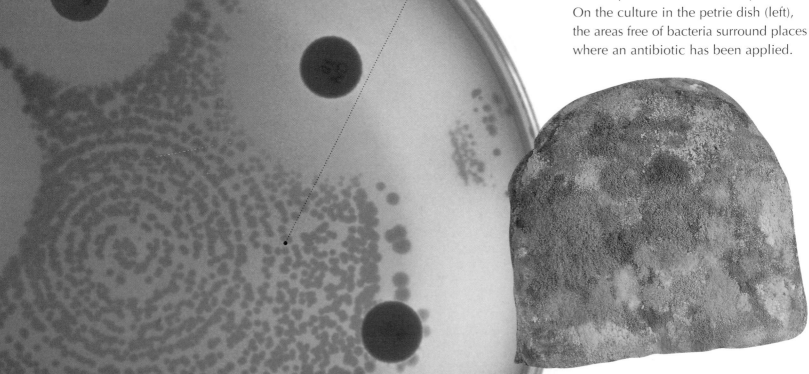

Bacteria killed
by antibiotic

Bacteria unaffected
by antibiotic

Brain Games

THE MISSING PICTURE

Trace the pieces of this jigsaw puzzle (below) onto a sheet of oaktag—colored on one side only so you know which way up the pieces go—and cut them out. Now put them back together. It is much harder to do a jigsaw in which shapes, rather than pictures, are the only visual clues for fitting the pieces together.

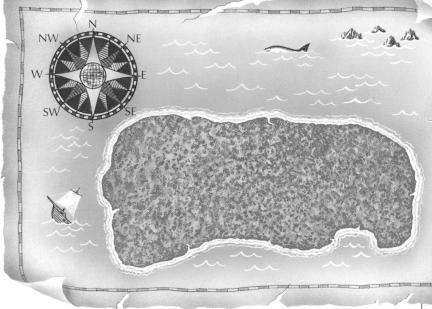

Cave   Forest   Camp   Mountain   Hill   Footprint

ISLAND MYSTERY

A mysterious footprint has been found somewhere on a desert island, but where? Make a map that shows the location of all the symbols above, using the information given here. Day one: Today we went into the forest in the corner of the island NE of our ship-wreck on the nearest part of the coast. The forest surrounds a cave. Day two: We have found a sandy cove in the SE of the island, and have pitched camp there. Day three: From our camp we can see a range of coastal mountains due west. The tallest is visible from the hill just north of our camp. Day four: We have found a footprint just north of the mountains. We are not alone! (See the Answers pages to check your map.)

TESTING SINGLE SENSES

It is much more difficult to identify things just by feel or smell than by sight alone. Here is a game to test the sense of touch (right). Take apart an object such as a pepper mill and put the pieces into a bag. Blindfold a friend and ask him or her to identify the object and then put the pieces back together without taking them out of the bag. To test your powers of smell, try while blindfolded to identify flowers or food by their scent alone.

TOUCHING WITH SPOONS

Here the missing links are sight and sensitive touch. Blindfold a friend and give him or her two spoons. Then ask your friend to identify household objects that you put in front of them by "feeling" them with the spoons. It isn't easy!

Getting Stuck and Thinking Sideways

For ages people were stuck with the idea that a flying machine had to be lighter than air if it was to fly!

APROBLEM MAY SEEM IMPOSSIBLE not because you don't know enough, but because your imagination is limited by other things you do know, or by false assumptions. But it is possible to escape such limitations just by "thinking sideways." This is called "lateral thinking." Many great inventions were thought of in this way, including the first successful flying machine. It was invented in 1903 by two American brothers, Wilbur and Orville Wright, who realized that a machine that was heavier than air could fly if only it could be made to move fast enough.

Brain Games

THE NINE-TREES PROBLEM

Mary has been sent to collect apples from the orchard on her bicycle (left). With the extra weight in her basket, she finds it difficult to turn corners and prefers to move in straight lines, making as few turns as possible. After a lot of thought, she thinks of a way to visit all the trees while making only three turns on her bicycle. How does she do it? Could you do better? (The Answers pages give one solution.)

AMAZING MIND READER

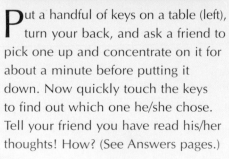

Put a handful of keys on a table (left), turn your back, and ask a friend to pick one up and concentrate on it for about a minute before putting it down. Now quickly touch the keys to find out which one he/she chose. Tell your friend you have read his/her thoughts! How? (See Answers pages.)

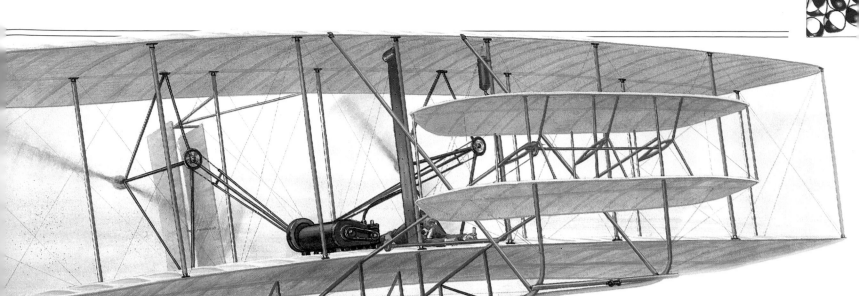

FLYING HIGH

The world's first successful airplane, *Flyer 1*, took to the air on December 17, 1903, and flew 98 feet (30 m) before landing. Two propellers were mounted behind the wings to push the plane forward. The pilot lay in a cradle on the lower wing next to the engine.

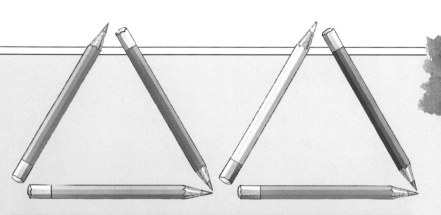

TWO TRIANGLES INTO EIGHT

These two triangles have been made using six pencils (above). Can you arrange them so that they make four triangles of any size? Easy? Now make four equal-size triangles! Can you also make eight uneven-size triangles? Don't look up the answer on the Answers pages until you have tried all three.

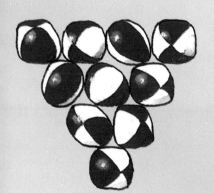

THE TEN-BALL TRIANGLE

By moving only three balls, change the triangle on the far left, with the line of four balls at the bottom, to the shape of the triangle on the left, with the line of four balls at the top. (The answer is on the Answers pages.)

TOO SHORT TO REACH

Elizabeth is trying to tie two pieces of string together, but she can't reach both of them at once (above). Suddenly, she realizes how to do it. The only things she has with her are a pair of scissors, a pencil, some tape, and a small jar of glue—as well as the squirrel! How does she solve the problem with lateral thinking? (See the Answers pages for one solution.)

Aha! Now I've Got It!

Some problems are solved with "a flash of inspiration." Even animals have these moments of brilliance.

A NEW IDEA MAY COME TO YOU very suddenly, but it does not come out of thin air. It comes because you already have all kinds of information, and suddenly you see a way to put the pieces together. "Aha!" you think, "now I've got it!" Sultan the chimpanzee had a flash of inspiration like this when he made a tool long enough to reach some fruit outside his cage. But before he had the idea of using the tool to reach the fruit, he had already spent a lot of time playing with bamboo sticks and fitting them together for fun. The Brain Games on these two pages may give you the same "Aha!" feeling he had when you do them.

CHICKEN-FOX-CORN

A farmer is on his way to market with a chicken, a fox, and a sack of corn (below). Before he reaches town, he has to cross a river, but his little rowboat is only big enough to hold him and one other thing at a time. Chickens eat corn and foxes eat chickens! How can he transport the chicken, the fox and the corn to the other side of the river without ever leaving the fox alone with the chicken or the chicken alone with the corn? (See Answers pages.)

SULTAN'S BRIGHT IDEA　▲

Sultan was given a stick that was long enough to reach a second stick outside his cage, but not long enough to reach a third stick or the pile of fruit a bit farther away. Eventually, he realized that he could use the first stick to reach the second one, and by joining the two together he could reach the third stick. With all three sticks joined together he could then reach the fruit!

COINS INTO CUPS

Can you put all eleven counters—or coins—(above) into three cups so that there is an odd number of counters in each cup? Easy? Now do it again using only ten counters. (You will groan at the answer on the Answers pages!)

TRUTHFUL AND UNTRUTHFUL TWINS

There are twins at a fork in the road (above). One always tells the truth, the other always tells lies, but you don't know which is which. One road leads to disaster, the other to safety. You can find out which is the safe road to take by asking either twin just one question. What question should you ask? (See Answers pages.)

PUZZLE DISKS

Place four disks of progressively smaller size in one of three spaces, as shown below (you could use four coins of different sizes or cut counters out of cardboard). Moving one disk at a time, and without placing a larger disk on top of a smaller one, move the pile of disks—still arranged by size with the smallest one on top—into one of the other spaces. The Answers pages reveal all.

Thinking Like a Scientist

Scientists solve problems in much the same way as the rest of us. But they focus on problems that no one has solved before.

A SCIENTIST DOES TWO EQUALLY important things. One is to come up with new ideas based on long-term study and research. The other is to test these ideas carefully before letting other people make use of them. The Austrian zoologist Konrad Lorenz, shown here, found that chicks or goslings that he hatched in an incubator followed him as if he were their mother. He believed this was because they "imprint" (memorize) the first moving thing they see after they hatch. This idea has been tested many times by scientists. They have found that chicks will imprint on all kinds of odd things, from a shoe box to a teddy bear! The Brain Games below enable you to make your own scientific discoveries and then test them.

Brain Games

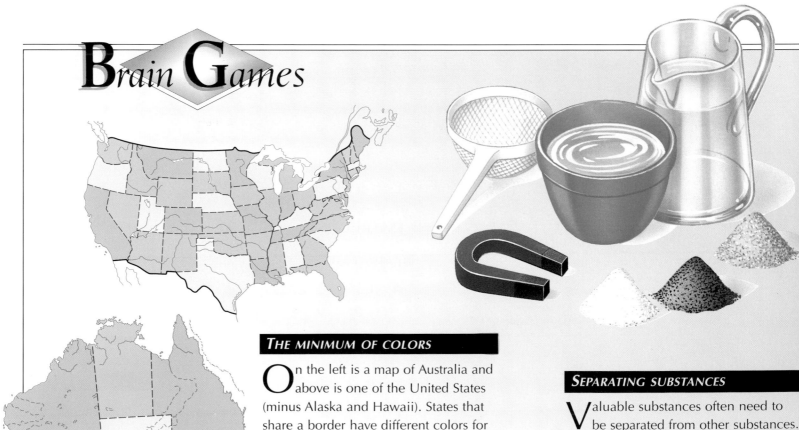

THE MINIMUM OF COLORS

On the left is a map of Australia and above is one of the United States (minus Alaska and Hawaii). States that share a border have different colors for clarity. Australia can be colored with a minimum of three colors. The U.S. needs four. Can you invent a map that **needs** five colors? (See the Answers pages.)

SEPARATING SUBSTANCES

Valuable substances often need to be separated from other substances. How could you separate a mixture of sawdust, salt, and iron filings (above), using only water and the tools shown? (See the Answers pages.)

MISTAKEN FOR MOM! ◄

Konrad Lorenz swims in a pool with the goslings who mistook him for their mother because he was the first moving thing they saw when they hatched from an incubator. In order to survive, goslings need to identify their mother from other geese the moment they hatch. Human babies take much longer.

MAKE A PAPER WING

Can you design a simple wing that actually lifts when air flows over it, from just a sheet of paper, a pencil, and some tape or glue (above)? Think about the shape of a real wing in cross-section. Is it wider at one end than the other? Experiment with different shapes. (One suggestion on the Answers pages.)

A DISPLACEMENT GAME

Mix two separate solutions of salt in water, making one much stronger than the other (left). How can you measure the relative amount of salt in each without separating the salt from the water? Hint: All you need is a pencil and weight. See the Answers pages.

PUTTING THE COLORS BACK INTO LIGHT

White light from the sun makes a rainbow when it shines through rain. Another way to separate the colors that make up white light is to shine a thin beam of sunlight through a prism or a glass of water. To get a beam, cut a hole in some cardboard, hold it next to a window, and close the curtains, except around the hole in the cardboard. Using two prisms, you can mix the colors to get white light again. How? (See the Answers pages.) If you don't have any prisms, you can get a similar effect by coloring a piece of card-board with the colors of the rainbow and spinning it. Draw stripes from the center to the edge of the card-board all the way around. Twist the string and let it untwist quickly so the disk spins.

Beam of light

Words and Pictures

People "see" their thoughts in their mind's eye in an extraordinary range of different ways. How do you visualize your thoughts?

SOME PEOPLE THINK IN WORDS AND NUMBERS, others in pictures, or a combination of pictures, words, and numbers. Some "hear" the words or numbers in their heads as they think (they talk to themselves mentally), others "see" words or numbers in colors or spread out in space. Some think without either words or pictures. These differences help us to understand why equally clever people can be good at very different things. They also explain why people have different types of dreams—some silent, others full of words, some in color, others colorless. Albert Einstein, one of the greatest scientists of all time, was famous for thinking in pictures. His ideas started to develop when he was a teenager and he imagined what it would be like to sit on a beam of light and move at the speed of light. He changed all our ideas about space, time, matter, and energy, and his work led to nuclear power and the invention of the atomic bomb.

$$E = mc^2$$

ENERGY equals mass times the speed of light squared

Brain Games

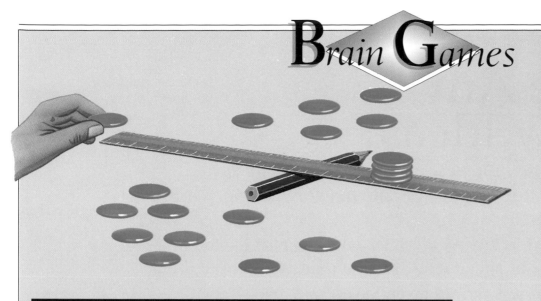

A PROBLEM OF BALANCE

Make a scale with a ruler and thick pencil (left). Put a few coins of the same denomination on one side and challenge a friend to balance them by putting a different number of the same coins on the other side. The friend will need to guess exactly where to put the coins. If he or she makes a mistake, don't allow corrections. Instead, make up a new problem. Do you "see" the answer or calculate it? (Calculation method on the Answers pages.)

THE DIFFICULTIES OF DESCRIBING

The twin brothers below look very much alike. Ignoring shirt color, which changes daily, how many subtle differences in their features can you spot? Try describing the differences in words and by drawing them as pictures. The police use both methods. Which are you better at? If you had to explain to someone the difference between a right-handed and a left-handed spiral staircase, would you do it in words or pictures? (Pictures on the Answers pages).

CROSSWISE

Arrange these pieces (right) to make a cross. You may find this harder if you are someone who thinks in words, not pictures. (See the Answers pages.)

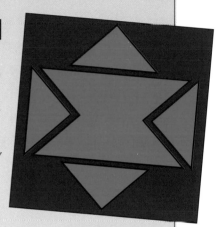

DR. DOLITTLE'S ANIMAL HOUSE

Dr. Dolittle says that in his house (below) all the animals except two are cats, all except two are dogs and all except two are rabbits. How many animals are in the house? (See the Answers pages.) Are you thinking in words or pictures or some other way? Give the problem to your friends and ask them how they solved it.

SAFE SWORDS

Which of these five swords, labeled A to E (left), will fit into scabbards 1 to 5 and which will not? Do you "picture" why they do not fit? Or do you think the answer in words? There are only four basic shapes that will fit into a scabbard. Three of them are shown here. What is the fourth? (See the Answers pages.)

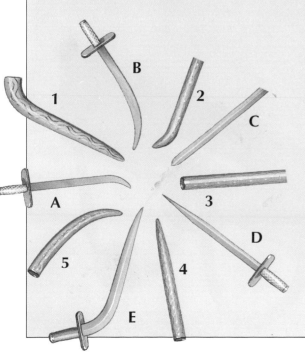

Are There Any Really New Ideas?

Most ideas that seem new are only new combinations of old ideas. Really new ideas are very rare and most people never have one.

THE AMERICAN SCIENTIST THOMAS EDISON, who invented motion pictures, the electric light bulb, sound recording and probably more things than anyone else in history, described invention as "99% perspiration and 1% inspiration." Most of the perspiration comes from thinking about old ideas and finding new uses for them. People in the Stone Age learned how to cook, probably from finding charred meat or vegetables after a forest fire. Since then many new ways of cooking have been invented, but they all make use of heat. Other people may think that our ideas are original, but only because they do not know where the ideas came from. The Brain Games below all make use of ideas found elsewhere in the book.

Brain Games

FIND THE HIDDEN OBJECTS!

There are ten hidden objects in this picture of a football game (left). Can you find the following: a flag, a large pair of glasses, a microphone, a bottle of ketchup, a large glass, a fork, the number 4, a hammer, a hiking boot, and a tennis ball. (See the Answers pages.)

MOVING THE BEAD, LIKE MAGIC!

Make this simple puzzle from a piece of thick cardboard, some string, and a bead or ring (right). How can you move the bead from the loop on the right to the loop on the left without untying the string? (See the Answers pages.)

COOKING WITH HEAT

Fire—the only method of cooking food in the Stone Age—emits "radiant" heat, which is absorbed by the surface of the food. By a process called conduction, it then heats the inside of the food. Twentieth-century microwave ovens send out a different form of radiant heat that penetrates deeper into the food, heating the inside directly.

CORRECT THE SUM IN NO MOVES

The sum in Roman numerals below is incorrect. How can you correct it without moving any of the pencils? (See Answers pages.)

X | + | = = X

ODDS OR EVENS?

Throw a handful of coins (or cardboard disks, green on one side, yellow on the other) onto a table (below). Count the number of heads (or greens). If it is an odd number, ask a friend to turn over pairs of coins—either two heads or two tails (yellows) or one of each—until he/she gets an even number. If you start with an even number, keep turning until you get an odd number. (Think about the problem before turning to the Answers pages.)

TIE THE KNOT

Hold one end of a piece of string in each hand (right). Now tie a knot in the string without letting go of either end. (Try it on your friends before turning to the Answers pages.)

TWELVE-STRAW PROBLEM

Using twelve straws (left), make six equal-sided squares. You may need to think sideways if you get stuck! (Turn to the Answers pages as a last resort.)

Answers

FILLING KNOWLEDGE GAPS   PAGE 6

Square = 3, circle = 2, triangle = 4, star = 5. The missing number is 14. To find the missing number without cracking the code, subtract the sum of the numbers down the side (35) from the sum of the numbers along the bottom (49).

WHICH SWITCH?   PAGE 6

Turn on the first switch and leave it on for two minutes before turning it off. Then turn on the next switch and leave it on for just 15 seconds before turning it off. Now feel the three light bulbs. The hottest bulb will be connected to the first switch you tried, the cooler one to the second and the cold one to the unused switch.

FIND THE QUICKEST ROUTE   PAGE 7

To work out the time it takes to get from one point to the next, divide the distance by the speed. The quickest route is this one: Home to f (5 m ÷ 2 mph = 2.5 hours); f to g (5 m ÷ 3 mph = 1.67 hours); g to red flag (15 m ÷ 2 mph = 7.5 hours); red flag to blue flag (8 m ÷ 5 mph = 1.6 hours). But it would be quicker to send out two separate parties to the two sites.

WHAT IS THE LONGEST SPAN?   PAGE 9

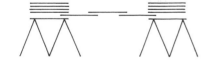

Hint: Put small weights such as coins on the cards to strengthen the bridge.

DESIGN A SPINNER   PAGE 9

Paper spinner   *Nature's helicopter*

A CODING DEVICE   PAGE 9

On the inner ring of the disc, read the letter one (or more) spaces to the right of the letter on the outer ring.

SALTY, SWEET, SOUR OR BITTER?   P.11

The map of your tongue should look something like this one. SA = salty; SO = sour; SW = sweet and BI = bitter.

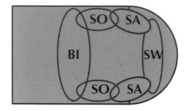

WHAT IS THE MISSING CARD?   PAGE 11

You only need to look through the pack three times to work out the missing card. The first time, count all the black cards. If there are 25 you know the missing card is black; if there are 26 you know it is red. If the missing card is black, count all the spades. If there are 13 you know the missing card is a club; if there are 12 you know it is a spade. Finally, when you know the suit, go through the suit to see which one is missing. Count aces as one, jacks as 11, queens as 12, and kings as 13. Subtract the numbers from 91 to leave the number of the missing card.

RECOGNITION   PAGE 11

The three objects are, clockwise from the top: a cheese grater, a pepper mill, and an electric hair dryer.

CRYPTARITHMETIC   PAGE 13

If X = 5, then W = 0, T = 1, S = 8 and J = 2.

MATCHING FACES   PAGE 13

The three pairs are: 1 and 5; 3 and 4; 2 and 6.

READING BAD HANDWRITING   PAGE 13

The chemical formulae written in bad handwriting are: $Fe_4[Fe(CN)_6]_3$, $Na_2SiO_4 \cdot xH_2O$ and $CaSO_4 \cdot \frac{1}{2}H_2O$.

CRACK THE PRICE CODE   PAGE 13

L = 0, M = 1, N = 2, K = 3, P = 4, Q = 6, R = 7, S = 8, T = 9.

WHICH BARBER?   PAGE 14

John should go to the barber with the bad haircut. If each barber cuts the other one's hair, the one with the bad haircut must be the good barber!

RED AND BLUE STICKERS   PAGE 15

If one person had been given a red sticker, the other one would see it and know that his/her own sticker was blue. If neither person reacts immediately, they must both have blue stickers.

MAKING CONNECTIONS   PAGE 16

You can press any two switches to make the star-shaped light come on.

NUMBERS GAME   PAGE 16

E.

ATTENTION TO DETAIL   PAGE 17

Star = 20, square = 30, oval = 49, rectangle = 30. There are 68 balls altogether.

SPOT THE DIFFERENCE   PAGE 17

WHAT COMES NEXT?   PAGE 17

The next shape in the sequence is 3. The shape that completes the box is D.

HIDDEN TRIANGLES   PAGE 19

We found 21!

LEFT, RIGHT, LEFT?   PAGE 19

1 = R, 2 = L, 3 = L, 4 = R, 5 = L, 6 = R, 7 = L, 8 = L, 9 = R, 10 = L, 11 = L, 12 = L, 13 = R, 14 = L, 15 = R, 16 = R, 17 = R, 18 = R.

QUICK SORTING — PAGE 21

All types of shape = 30.
Red shapes = 16. Green shapes =14.

Red triangles = 10. <u>Red triangles with dot = 4</u>; red triangles with dot and shadow = 1; red triangles with dot and no shadow = 3; <u>red triangles without dot = 6</u>; red triangles without dot but with shadow = 3; red triangles without dot and with no shadow = 3. **Red circles = 6.** <u>Red circles with dot = 2</u>; red circles with dot and shadow = 1, red circles with dot but no shadow = 1; <u>red circles without dot = 4</u>; red circles without dot but with shadow = 2; red circles without dot and with no shadow = 2. **Green triangles = 9;** <u>green triangles with dot = 5</u>; green triangles with dot and shadow = 4; green triangles with dot but no shadow = 1; <u>green triangles without dot = 4</u>; green triangles without dot but with shadow = 2; green triangles without dot and with no shadow = 2. **Green circles = 5;** <u>green circles with dot = 3</u>; green circles with dot and shadow = 1; green circles with dot but no shadow = 2; <u>green circles without dot = 2</u>; green circles without dot but with shadow = 1; green circles without dot and with no shadow = 1.

To make counting easier, draw a box for each possible combination and check off the appropriate boxes as you count.

STOP THE RULER — PAGE 21

Use the scale on the right-hand edge of this page to test your speed of reactions.

TURNING THE COGS — PAGE 22

A: both buckets go down. B: clockwise. C: counterclockwise.

SPELLING TEST — PAGE 23

Incorrectly! This word has 11 letters!

MAKING BOXES — PAGES 22/23

1 = B, 2 = G.

NEXT IN THE SEQUENCE — PAGE 23

On left: D. On right: C.

CHINESE WRITING — PAGE 25

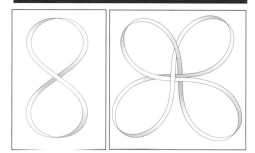

MAKE A CIRCLE IN THREE MOVES — P. 25

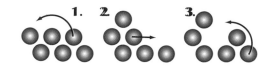

KNIGHT MOVES — PAGE 26

Move each piece in turn in a clockwise direction. After each piece has moved twice, the red knights will have changed places with the yellow knights.

MATCH THE ROTATED SHAPES — PAGE 26

First pair: B and C. Second pair: E and D. A and F do not match any of the other shapes.

ONE-SIDED PAPER — PAGE 27

WHAT KNOT? — PAGE 27

A is the slipknot.

GET UNKNOTTED — PAGE 27

Slide the part of the other person's string that passes *under* yours up to your wrist. Insert it through the loop around your wrist, from the arm toward the hand. Pass your hand under it and pull free.

WHO IS THE TALLEST? — PAGE 29

1 = Tom. 5 = Jack. Note that in the information you are given, Tom is not taller than anyone and no one is taller than Jack.

NEXT IN THE SEQUENCE — PAGE 29

Disk A is the next in the sequence.

GUESS-THE-CARD GAME — PAGE 29

The facedown card is number 9 — it is the sum of the numbers on the four cards surrounding it.

ARE YOUR WIRES CROSSED? — PAGE 29

If you try to run the pipes or cables outside the houses, the problem can't be solved! But if you think laterally and run them underneath or through the houses, there are a number of solutions. Here is one of them.

THE SHEEP PEN PUZZLE — PAGE 29

You only need two extra hurdles for the six new sheep. By adding an extra hurdle at each end of the pen, you double its size.

ISLAND MYSTERY — PAGE 31

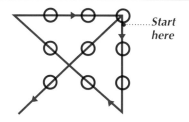

THE NINE-TREES PROBLEM — PAGE 32

Start here

AMAZING MINDREADER — PAGE 32

The key that the friend held in his or her hand will be noticeably warmer than all the others.

TWO TRIANGLES INTO EIGHT — PAGE 33

THE TEN-BALL TRIANGLE   PAGE 33

Move the two outside balls on the bottom row up two rows and move the top ball down to the center bottom.

TOO SHORT TO REACH   PAGE 33

She tied the scissors to the string from the tree and let it swing. Then she held the end of the string attached to the pole, and when the other string swung toward her, she caught it and tied the two strings together.

CHICKEN-FOX-CORN   PAGE 34

1. The farmer takes the chicken across and leaves it. 2. He comes back and takes the fox across, but brings the chicken back with him. 3. He leaves the chicken and takes the corn across, which he leaves with the fox. 4. He comes back and collects the chicken!

COINS INTO CUPS   PAGE 35

Put five, three and two counters into different cups. Then put the cup with three counters into the cup with two, so that it contains five counters!

TRUTHFUL AND UNTRUTHFUL TWINS P. 35

Ask either twin which road the other would say is safe; take the other road.

PUZZLE DISKS   PAGE 35

On the first move, and all subsequent odd-numbered moves, move the smallest piece in a clockwise direction. On even-numbered moves, make the only legal move not involving the smallest disk.

SEPARATING SUBSTANCES   PAGE 36

Use the magnet to separate the iron filings from the sawdust. Place the rest of the mixture in the water, and skim off the sawdust, which will float. Now put the water in a warm place until it has evaporated; this will leave the salt behind in the bowl.

THE MINIMUM OF COLORS   PAGE 36

Mathematicians have only just proved that it can't be done!

MAKING A PAPER WING   PAGE 37

Wings give more lift if the upper surface is more curved than the lower surface.

A DISPLACEMENT GAME   PAGE 37

Weight one end of the pencil and float it upright in unsalted water. Mark the waterline on the pencil. Then float it in the two salt solutions, marking the waterline each time. The increase in the length of pencil above the water is proportional to the amount of salt in the water.

PUTTING THE COLORS. . .   PAGE 37

To mix separated colors of light with two prisms, hold one point-up and the other point-down so that they bend the light in opposite directions.

A PROBLEM OF BALANCE   PAGE 39

The ruler will balance when the weight multiplied by its distance from the balance point is the same on each side.

THE DIFFICULTIES OF DESCRIBING P.39

Boys: There are four subtle differences in their features. Boy in blue has a thicker top lip and thinner eyebrows. Boy in red has wider ears and a mole.
Spiral staircases: As you go up the stairs, the central column is either on your right or your left.

CROSSWISE   PAGE 39

DR. DOLITTLE'S ANIMAL HOUSE P.39

There are only three animals in the house (one of each kind).

SAFE SWORDS   PAGE 39

B fits into 5, C into 3, and D into 4. A and E do not fit into anything. The only other type that will fit is one with an even twist, which can be "screwed" into the scabbard (right).

FIND THE HIDDEN OBJECTS   PAGE 40

MOVING THE BEAD, LIKE MAGIC! P.40

Push the bead up through the horizontal loop and hold it against the slit. Pull the horizontal loop through the slit from the back to the front, dragging both vertical loops with it. Pass the bead along the horizontal loop and through the two vertical loops. Return the horizontal loop to its original position and pull the bead through it until it hangs down on the other vertical loop.

CORRECT THE SUM IN NO MOVES P.41

Turn the page around 180 degrees and look again!

ODDS OR EVENS?   PAGE 41

It can't be done! Turning two of the same adds or subtracts an even number, leaving odd numbers odd, and even numbers even. Turning two different ones, leaves the number of heads and tails the same.

TIE THE KNOT   PAGE 41

Fold your arms before holding the string! Unfolding your arms will tie the knot.

TWELVE-STRAW PROBLEM   PAGE 4

Make a cube with four square sides, a square top and a square bottom. (You will need glue!)

Glossary

Antibiotics
Chemical substances—either produced by various microorganisms such as fungi or made synthetically—which are capable of destroying bacteria.

Antiseptic
A substance that stops the growth or action of microorganisms, especially in or on living tissue.

Bacteria
Single-celled microorganisms that colonize all living bodies, plants, water, soil and so on, and can cause disease.

Brain function
The action of the brain that enables us to feel sensations and emotions, to think and to remember.

Character
A letter, number or symbol that has a well-understood meaning.

Code
A system of letters or symbols that represent other letters, symbols or specific information. A coded message is only understandable to a person or machine that knows the associated information; used for secret communication.

Competition
People working toward a common objective, but trying to outdo each other.

Cooperation
People working together in harmony to achieve a common objective.

Cryptarithmetic
Arithmetic using coded numbers.

Displacement
The weight or volume displaced by a floating object. Because a floating object displaces its own weight of liquid, it will float higher in a heavier liquid than in a light one.

Force
Any influence that makes a motionless object move; or prevents a moving object from continuing in a straight line; or causes an object to change its speed, i.e. to accelerate or decelerate.

Friction
The force exerted when one surface moves across another in the opposite direction.

Hand-to-eye coordination
Visual control of hand movements.

Imprint
The tendency of some young birds and mammals to follow the first thing they see after they are born.

Incubator
A machine for keeping eggs warm until they hatch.

Lateral thinking
Thinking in an unconventional or unorthodox way, often described as "thinking sideways."

Legal moves
A move that is allowed by the rules of a game such as chess.

Lubrication
A substance such as oil that reduces friction and allows two or more objects to keep moving, even though they are in contact with each other.

Memory
A function of the brain that enables us to remember.

Personality
The sum total of our likes, interests, abilities and mental characteristics. Personality is what makes each individual unique.

Programmed
Instructed to respond in a particular way. The term is usually applied to a computer that has been given instructions in a coded form that it can read.

Radiant heat
Sending out heat (electromagnetic waves) by radiation. X-rays, light, radiant heat, microwaves and radio waves are all electromagnetic waves of progressively longer wavelengths.

Scientist
A person who uses the scientific methods of observing, experimenting, developing theories and then testing the theories to arrive at a conclusion.

Sensation
An impression perceived through one of the five main senses: sight, sound, touch, smell and taste.

Topology
The study of the shapes of things.

Vocation
A desire to follow a particular career such as teaching or medicine.

Zoologist
A scientist who studies animals.

Index

Numbers in *italics* refer to captions.

J
153.42
HOW   Think about it!

Howarth, Ian

	DATE DUE		
HIC ● JUN 1999			